# A CALL TO PRAYER

In a time of uncer~~tain~~ illness, it is nat~~u~~ . When we rea~~c~~ with gratitude on the revelation ~~~ed.

In the Gospels Jesus reassures us that ~~all~~ prayers will be answered when they are offered with certain characteristics and attitudes.

"When you pray, go to your room, close the door, and pray to your Father in private" (Matthew 6:6). In the parable of the Pharisee and Tax Collector, Jesus clarifies for us how we must pray. "Two people went up to the temple area to pray; one was a Pharisee and the other was a tax collector. The Pharisee took up his position and spoke this prayer to himself, 'O God, I thank you that I am not like the rest of humanity – greedy, dishonest, adulterous – or even like this tax collector. I fast twice a week, and I pay tithes on my whole income.' But the tax collector stood off at a distance and would not even raise his eyes to heaven but beat his breast and prayed, 'O God, be merciful to me a sinner.' I tell you, the latter went home justified, not the former; for everyone who exalts himself will be humbled, and the one who humbles himself will be exalted" (Luke 18:10-14).

Throughout the Gospel, Jesus teaches us to pray with faith, sincerity, trust, and perseverance. Jesus tells us to place ourselves in a humble attitude of listening in order to hear God's answer to our prayers. When we pray, we must conclude each prayer as Jesus did: "Father, if it is your will, take this cup from me; yet not my will but yours be done" (Luke 22:42).

Through this book with its scripture texts and artwork, we want to remind you that Jesus always hears and answers our prayers, especially in times of duress.

Our faith teaches us that prayer is the way we learn to know and love God personally. When we pray, we realize that we are never alone or abandoned. Prayer enables us to experience comfort and peace because we know that God loves us and that He is always ready to give us what we need.

*The Authors*

*"Ask, and you will receive. Seek, and you will find. Knock, and it will be opened to you. For the one who asks, receives. The one who seeks, finds. The one who knocks, enters" (Matthew 7:7-18).*

Illness and healing are reminders that ultimately life is in God's hands. Illness and healing are also signs of Jesus' grace and mercy. Our Divine Lord took up His Cross and became weak in order to give meaning to suffering. He assumed a fallen human nature and redeemed it by fulfilling the promise of the Resurrection through His Passion and Death.

<u>Ask, and You Will Receive</u> will encourage those who are suffering to confidently speak with "Jesus the Listener" and share with Him their concerns. Having endured suffering Himself, Jesus is always ready to answer our prayers and be "God with us."

How grateful we should be to Mary, the Mother of God, who by her humble acceptance of God's will, brought Jesus into the world. May the Mother of Sorrows be our example during times of distress. May she fortify us with her maternal protection and love as we stand with her at the foot of the Cross before "Jesus the Listener".

Many people who lived in Jesus' time asked and received healing. May all who use this prayer book feel the touch of Jesus' hand and hear the sound of His voice. And may His healing power bring you hope and new life.

John Cardinal O'Connor
July 26, 1996

*To Fernando Bologna*


*who knew suffering and the grace of God*


*that gave him strength and courage.*

Nihil Obstat:  Francis J. McAree, S.T.D.
Censor Librorum

Imprimi Potest:  Very Rev. Robert Joerger, C.P.
Provincial of St. Paul of the Cross Province

Imprimatur:  + Patrick Sheridan, D.D.
Vicar General, Archdiocese of New York
June 3, 1996

*The Nihil Obstat and Imprimatur are official declarations that a book or pamphlet is free of doctrinal or moral error.  No implication is contained therein that those who have granted the Nihil Obstat and Imprimatur agree with the contents, opinions or statements expressed.*

**ISBN 0-9684816-0-4**

Printed in Canada
St. Joseph Printing, Concord, Ontario


Artwork by Mary Celestino
Layout by Piero Galluzzo


Jesus the Listener:
Sculpture created by Anthony Antonios
Foundry, Ranieri Sculpture Casting
Photography by Lou Manna of The Manna Group, Inc.


All Scripture passages are taken from the Saint Joseph Edition of
The New American Bible, 1970.

# INTRODUCTION

*"Look toward me, and have pity on me, for I am alone and afflicted. Relieve the troubles of my heart, and bring me out of my distress. Put an end to my affliction and my suffering, and take away all my sins" (Psalm 25:16-18).*

uffering has been with us from the very beginning of human existence. People have always looked to God for help. In the words of the Psalmist, we discover a heartfelt plea for relief and salvation. We also hear a confidence in God that we must all have, especially when we find ourselves in times of need and stress.

Our Christian tradition has presented Jesus as the ultimate answer of the Father to our needs. Through the centuries, the mission of Jesus has been presented in many ways, each revealing a particular truth of his divinity and humanity.

In this book Jesus is presented as The Listener, emphasizing that He is never far away from us, that He is always attentive to our suffering, and that He hears and answers our prayers.

*The Authors*

# CONTENTS

# CHAPTER I

## "THE FOOL SAYS IN HIS HEART, 'THERE IS NO GOD'" (PSALM 14:1).

There are many of us who under difficult situations choose to complain against God and refuse to consider that there might be positive meaning in our adversities. There are others who look at the same adversities, and in spite of everything, find reason to thank God for them.

"You changed my mourning into dancing; you took off my sackcloth and clothed me with gladness. That my soul might sing praise to you without ceasing; O Lord, my God, forever will I give you thanks" (Psalm 30:12-13).

When tragedy or sorrow faces us, many of us do tend to say, at some point, "There is no God." We are tempted to lose heart and faith.

The Bible teaches us that suffering and death came into the world as a result of original sin. It also tells us that a humble and trusting attitude in God at times of suffering can strengthen our fidelity in God's providential plan of salvation.

Our finite minds cannot totally understand the mystery of suffering; thus it always causes doubt and confusion.

"His disciples asked him, 'Rabbi, was it his sin or that of his parents that caused him to be born blind?' 'Neither,' answered Jesus: 'It was no sin, either of this man or of his parents. Rather, it was to let God's works show forth in him'" (John 9:2-3).

hat God permits suffering in our lives is a mystery. At the same time, suffering is a sign of God's love for us, as well as healing is. We see this very clearly in the life of Jesus. "For whom the Lord loves he reproves, and he chastises the son he favors" (Proverbs 3:12).

Jesus is God's answer to our suffering and the need for spiritual and physical healing. Whenever Jesus cured, it was first to heal spiritually, either by giving or increasing faith. Spiritual healing meant that the relationship between the person and God the Father was restored. The person would then be better able to carry the cross that God had allowed to be present in his or her life. The person would be able to live with joy and peace, and find meaning in life even in the midst of suffering.

When we pray, our first priority is to ask Jesus for spiritual healing. When we are willing to do God's will, even though we find ourselves confronted with the reality of suffering, we will receive the necessary strength from God to overcome suffering. The Apostle Paul reassures us of this truth: "In him who is the source of my strength, I have strength for everything" (Philippians 4:13).

Do we really believe in this mysterious God? Do we trust in his love and faithfulness to us? "See, upon the palms of my hands I have written your name" (Isaiah: 49:16). God our Creator listens attentively and has the power to answer our prayers. "The Lord has eyes for the just, and ears for their cry" (Psalm 34:16).

he Lord knows us by name because He created us. "He tells the number of the stars; He calls each by name" (Psalm 147:4). He loves us with an infinite love, and we belong to him. "With age-old love I have loved you; so I have kept my mercy toward you" (Jeremiah 31:3). The Lord gives us everything we need, and yes, even the miraculous.

"Ask, and you will receive. Seek, and you will find. Knock, and it will be opened to you. For the one who asks, receives. The one who seeks, finds. The one who knocks, enters. Would one of you hand his son a stone when he asks for a loaf, or a poisonous snake when he asks for a fish? If you, with all your sins, know how to give your children what is good, how much more will your heavenly Father give good things to anyone who asks him!" (Matthew 7:7-11).

The Son of God spoke these words and showed his love for us by accepting the Will of his Father and dying on the cross.

Although suffering is evil and not from God, every time we look at a crucifix, we can view suffering with another insight. We can see the compassion and mercy of a loving Father. The Father chose suffering as the means to overcome evil and death in the world to bring about the salvation of all his children through the Resurrection of his Son. Only by understanding this redemptive aspect of suffering can we face the crucifix and discover the truth of the words: "The fool says in his heart, 'There is no God'" (Psalm 14:1).

# CHAPTER II

## THE JESUS THE LISTENER CRUCIFIX

*"As for myself, brothers, when I came to you I did not come proclaiming God's testimony with any particular eloquence or 'wisdom.' No, I determined that while I was with you I would speak of nothing but Jesus Christ and him crucified. When I came among you it was in weakness and fear, and with much trepidation. My message and my preaching had none of the persuasive force of 'wise' argumentation, but the convincing power of the Spirit. As a consequence, your faith rests not on the wisdom of men but on the power of God"* *(1 Corinthians 2:1-5).*

 hese words of St. Paul the Apostle speak not only of his own personal faith in Jesus Crucified, but also of the fundamental truth that the crucifix is the center of salvation history. The crucifix represents "the greatest and most wonderful act of God's love" (St. Paul of the Cross).

In the Old Testament, the experiences of the Patriarchs Abraham, Jacob, Isaac, and Joseph exemplify God's loving plan to grant redemption. "In you our fathers trusted; they trusted, and you delivered them. To you they cried, and they escaped; in you they trusted, and they were not put to shame" (Psalm 22:5-6).

he lives of men and women of faith, such as Moses, David, Judith, Ester, and Ruth are a great reassurance to us because of God's intervention in their suffering. They experienced confusion, uncertainty and trials, and yet, they were able to trust in the promises of a listening God. "They cried to the Lord in their distress; from their straits he rescued them. And he led them forth from darkness and gloom and broke their bonds asunder" (Psalm 107:13-14).

The greatest evidence of God's faithfulness to his promises and the surest guarantee that He is listening are visible in the crucifix.

Look at Jesus nailed to the cross, listening to our needs and pleading to the Father on our behalf. "Father, forgive them; they do not know what they are doing" (Luke 23:24). He is Jesus the Listener who heard the appeal of the Good Thief: "I assure you: this day you will be with me in paradise" (Luke 23:43). Jesus comforts us and reassures us that in his company, even our greatest suffering can be endured without losing hope.

*"Come to me, all you who are weary and find life burdensome, and I will refresh you. Take my yoke upon your shoulders and learn from me, for I am gentle and humble of heart. Your souls will find rest, for my yoke is easy and my burden light" (Matthew 11:28-30).*

# CHAPTER III

## THE CALL FROM DARKNESS

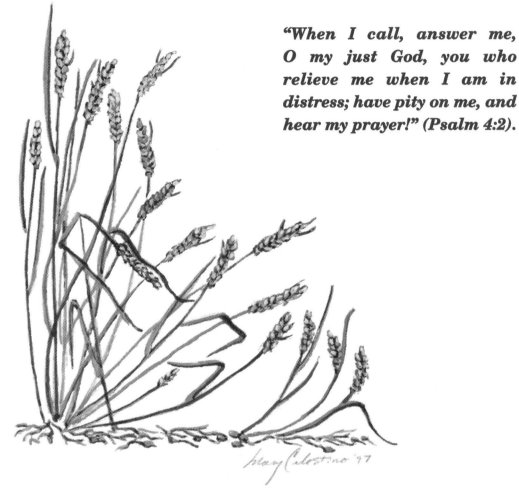

*"When I call, answer me, O my just God, you who relieve me when I am in distress; have pity on me, and hear my prayer!" (Psalm 4:2).*

very act of surrender done out of love for God and in union with the sufferings of Jesus on the cross is the source of new life. "I solemnly assure you, unless the grain of wheat falls to the earth and dies, it remains just a grain of wheat. But if it dies, it produces much fruit" (John 12:24).

We learn from Jesus that human suffering becomes the point of encounter with the Infinite God. And from the death of Jesus on the cross, God the Father reveals that He always favors the lonely, the abandoned, and the suffering. He brings them forth from the darkness into the light. We are never alone and never forgotten.

hrough our personal suffering, we share intimately with Jesus, and with each other, for indeed we are one body in Christ: "Just as each of us has one body with many members, and not all the members have the same function, so too we, though many, are one body in Christ and individually members one of another" (Romans 12:4-5).

St. Peter reminds us of our great call to intimacy with Jesus in suffering: "But if you put up with suffering for doing what is right, this is acceptable in God's eyes. It was for this you were called, since Christ suffered for you in just this way and left you an example, to have you follow in his footsteps. He did no wrong; no deceit was found in his mouth. When he was insulted, he returned no insult. When he was made to suffer, he did not counter with threats. Instead, he delivered himself up to the One who judges justly. In his own body he brought your sins to the cross, so that all of us, dead to sin, could live in accord with God's will. By his wounds you were healed. At one time you were straying like sheep, but now you have returned to the shepherd, the guardian of your souls" (1 Peter 2:20-25).

During illness and suffering, the Father offers us the chance to be a new creation through the power of the Holy Spirit. We become this new creation, not by our trying to solve the mystery of suffering, but by our sharing everything we are, our frailty and our hidden strengths with Jesus Crucified. Through our surrender to his will, we are transformed: "When you send forth your spirit, they are created, and you renew the face of the earth" (Psalm 104:30).

ny kind of suffering may plunge us into the darkness of anger, depression, and despair. But through our willing embrace of suffering in imitation of Jesus, we receive a new understanding of life.

Mary Magdalene came face to face with the reality of suffering and the consequent darkness and confusion that suffering caused in her life. But through her love of Jesus and her acceptance of the events that had taken place in her life, she experienced conversion and was brought from darkness to light. On Easter morning the Risen Lord spoke to her through the words of an angel: "Do not be frightened. I know you are looking for Jesus the crucified, but he is not here. He has been raised, exactly as he promised" (Matthew 28:5-6).

The Resurrection of Jesus shows us that all the chaos of this life has no power over our final destiny. One day Jesus will call all of us "from darkness into his marvelous light" (1 Peter 2:9).

# CHAPTER IV

## THINKING ABOUT LIFE

> *"The Lord will guard you from all evil; he will guard your life. The Lord will guard your coming and your going, both now and forever" (Psalm 121:7-8).*

ur most natural instinct is to want to live. We love life and we want to enjoy it. Even though life is something that we have received as a gift from God, many times we consider it to be our own private possession. We might even find it difficult to trust anyone else with the care of it, even God the Creator.

A time of illness and suffering brings us face to face with our inability to ultimately control life and to protect it. At a time such as this, the idea that an eternal and loving God is in charge of life and that He will take care of it and sustain it becomes comforting.

We usually think that the well-being of our bodies and the enhancement of our spiritual growth may come from an unexpected success, a new source of consolation, or even a miracle. But in God's mysterious plan, we discover that suffering and trials usually offer us the greatest opportunities for true healing and spiritual growth. The recognition of our frailty leads us to acknowledge and depend on the power and the love of God.

hen we treasure our physical life, we spend time and effort in protecting and enhancing it. Our faith teaches us that while earthly life is a precious and sacred gift, there is another dimension to life that is even more important, namely, our eternal life with God.

One of the most reassuring teachings of Jesus is that we are destined to live forever with God. "In my Father's house there are many dwelling places; otherwise, how could I have told you that I was going to prepare a place for you? I am indeed going to prepare a place for you, and then I shall come back to take you with me, that where I am you also may be" (John 14:2-3).

The loss of our immortal soul is a far greater misfortune than any illness, sorrow or human tragedy. "Whoever would save his life will lose it, but whoever loses his life for my sake will find it. What profit would a man show if he were to gain the whole world and destroy himself in the process? What can a man offer in exchange for his very self?" (Matthew 16:25-26).

Human suffering is part of life because of the fall into sin of our first parents Adam and Eve. God did not create suffering and death. Death and suffering are the results of sin. But because our God is a God of Life and because He wants us to be with him forever, He gave us his only-begotten Son to redeem us. "Yes, God so loved the world that he gave his only Son, that whoever believes in him may not die but may have eternal life" (John 3:16).

For this very reason, even in the midst of our suffering, we can daily say what the Church proclaims on Easter Vigil: "O happy fault, O necessary sin of Adam, which gained for us so great a Redeemer!" *(Easter Proclamation, Exsultet).*

# CHAPTER V

## THE GRACE OF PERSONAL DETACHMENT

*"Our soul waits for the Lord, who is our help and our shield, for in him our hearts rejoice; in his holy name we trust. May your kindness, O Lord, be upon us who have put our hope in you" (Psalm 33:20-22).*

 ur faith is of great value to us when it teaches: "Do not lay up for yourselves an earthly treasure. Moths and rust corrode; thieves break in and steal. Make it your practice instead to store up heavenly treasure, which neither moths nor rust corrode nor thieves break in and steal" (Matthew 6: 19-21).

Detachment is an absolutely necessary quality for our lives if we desire to grow to full spiritual maturity. Full spiritual maturity is the profound realization that we were created by a loving God, that we belong to him, and that we are destined to be with him forever.

eing with him forever is the very source of our happiness.

St. Augustine expresses this truth very beautifully in his famous book The Confessions: "You are great, O Lord, and greatly to be praised; great is your power and to your wisdom there is no limit. And man, who is a part of your creation, wishes to praise you, man who bears about within himself his mortality, who bears about within himself testimony to his sin and testimony that you resist the proud. Yet man, this part of your creation, wishes to praise you. You arouse him to take joy in praising you, for you have made us for yourself, and our heart is restless until it rests in you" (The Confessions, Book I, Chapter I).

Jesus is the greatest teacher of personal detachment. Even though Jesus is God, his life among us is intimately connected with doing the will of his Father. "Doing the will of him who sent me and bringing his work to completion is my food" (John 4:34).

*"I cannot do anything of myself. I judge as I hear, and my judgment is honest because I am not seeking my own will but the will of him who sent me" (John 5:30).*

he life and mission of Jesus, the very purpose of his coming to save us, were based on doing the will of the Father who sent him. "Because it is not to do my own will that I have come down from heaven, but to do the will of him who sent me" (John 6:38).

When we pray for personal detachment, we ought to align our will with that of the Father as Jesus did, with complete trust and humility: "Father, if it is your will, take this cup from me; yet not my will but yours be done" (Luke 22:42).

Detachment will always challenge us to sacrifice what we treasure the most. The Apostle Paul offered the Philippians an insight into the supreme detachment of Jesus: "Though he was in the form of God, he did not deem equality with God something to be grasped at. Rather, he emptied himself and took the form of a slave, being born in the likeness of men. He was known to be of human estate, and it was thus that he humbled himself, obediently accepting even death, death on a cross!" (Philippians 2:6-8).

This example of Jesus inspires us to practice personal detachment, especially when we are faced with suffering. By uniting our suffering with those of Jesus in his passion and death, our detachment will offer us the possibility of possessing ultimate happiness and joy. "Eye has not seen, ear has not heard, nor has it so much as dawned on man what God has prepared for those who love him" (1 Corinthians 2:9).

*"Those that sow in tears shall reap rejoicing" (Psalm 126:5).*

16

# CHAPTER VI

## A CALL TO FAITH

*"Taste and see how good the Lord is; happy the man who takes refuge in him" (Psalm 34:5).*

aith is a gift that God gives us at Baptism. Faith strengthens us to accept what we might find difficult to understand, such as suffering. Faith is the virtue that helps us to discover meaning to our lives. Faith gives us the power to accept with courage those events in our lives that are at odds with our human wisdom and knowledge, such as illness and death.

Because faith is a gift, it can be lost. In order to protect it, to make it grow, and to purify it, we need to pray. We need to be in contact with God, the source of faith. Whenever we pray, we exercise our Faith.

*"I assure you, if you had faith the size of a mustard seed, you would be able to say to this mountain, 'Move from here to there,' and it would move. Nothing would be impossible for you" (Matthew 17:20).*

veryone in the Gospels who came in touch with Jesus and asked him ~~~~~~~~ was always rewarded because ~~~~~~~~ lked on water. The Good Thief ~~~~~~~~ adise. The lepers were healed. The ce~~~~~~~~ lind Bartimacus received his sight. M~~~~~~~~ Lazarus restored to life.

We find the greatest example of faith in Mary our Blessed Mother. Throughout her life, Mary lived in faith. She never said "No" to God, even when following his will meant personal suffering, confusion, uncertainty, and trials. The Incarnation of God was possible because of Mary's "Yes" as an act of faith. "I am the servant of the Lord. Let it be done to me as you say" (Luke 1:38).

# CHAPTER VII

## PERSONAL FAITH IN THE ONE WHO LISTENS

*"A clean heart create for me, O God, and a steadfast spirit renew within me. Cast me not out from your presence, and your holy spirit take not from me. Give me back the joy of your salvation, and a willing spirit sustain in me" (Psalm 51:12-14).*

 od our Father, by allowing Jesus his only-begotten Son to be lifted on the cross, presents him as The Listener.

With his eyes fixed on us, Jesus the Listener expresses the mercy of a God-Man who loves us without counting the cost and who forgives without conditions. Jesus not only manifests the atrocious condition of a crucified man, but also the cruel reality of the effects of our sins.

By contemplating his holy face, we discover divine compassion, love, and forgiveness for our fallen human condition.

The passion of Jesus is God's greatest act of love. May this truth lead us to a greater awareness of our personal importance to God. We are each a masterpiece in his eyes for "God created man in his image; in the divine image he created him; male and female he created them" (Genesis 1:27).

*"The Lord is close to the brokenhearted; and those who are crushed in spirit he saves" (Psalm 34:19).*

Christ did not do away with suffering. He did not even wish to unveil to us entirely the mystery of suffering. He took suffering upon himself and this is enough to make you understand all its value. All of you who feel heavily the weight of the cross, you who are poor and abandoned, you who weep, you who are persecuted for justice, you who are ignored, you the unknown victims of suffering, take courage. You are the preferred children of the kingdom of God, the kingdom of hope, happiness and life. You are the brothers of the suffering Christ, and with him, if you wish, you are saving the world.

This is the Christian science of suffering, the only one which gives peace. Know that you are not alone, separated, abandoned, or useless. You have been called by Christ and are his living and transparent image. In his name, the Council salutes you lovingly, thanks you, assures you of the friendship and assistance of the Church and blesses you.

*Statements of the Ecumenical Council*
*December 8, 1965*

# CHAPTER VIII

"MASTER, TO WHOM SHALL WE GO?" (JOHN 6:68).

*"Then Job began to tear his cloak and cut off his hair. He cast himself prostrate upon the ground, and said, 'Naked I came forth from my mother's womb, and naked shall I go back again. The Lord gave and the Lord has taken away; blessed be the name of the Lord!' In all this Job did not sin, nor did he say anything disrespectful of God" (Job 1:20-22).*

he instinct and desire to protect and prolong life are present in all of us. And yet can we choose the time or the place to be born and to die?  Can we know the length of our lives? "Can any of you by worrying add a single moment to your life-span?" (Matthew 6:27).

When all the facts have been considered and all the possible answers heard, in extremely difficult situations, we can only come to one sensible conclusion – God is the source and the keeper of life. The Scripture abounds in examples of people who have faced torture, persecution, and even death, upholding this truth.

The Good Thief facing certain death says: "Jesus, remember me when you come into your kingdom" (Luke 23:42). He took the chance to trust in Jesus, and he received the answer he longed to hear: "Amen, I say to you, today you will be with me in Paradise" (Luke 23:43).

The woman caught in adultery was about to be stoned according to Jewish law. Jesus upheld her even though she was guilty. "Go, and from now on do not sin any more" (John 8:11).

The Apostle Peter walked on water at the invitation of Jesus. But when Peter began to sink, he cried out, "'Lord, save me!' Immediately Jesus stretched out his hand and caught him, and said to him, 'O you of little faith, why did you doubt?'" (Matthew 14:30-31).

"While he was still speaking, people from the synagogue official's house arrived and said, 'Your daughter has died; why trouble the teacher any longer?' Disregarding the message that was reported, Jesus said to the synagogue official, 'Do not be afraid; just have faith.' He did not allow anyone to accompany him inside except Peter, James, and John, the brother of James. When they arrived at the house of the synagogue official, he caught sight of a commotion, people weeping and wailing loudly. So he went in and said to them, 'Why this commotion and weeping? The child is not dead but asleep.' And they ridiculed him. Then he put them all out. He took along the child's father and mother and those who were with him and entered the room where the child was. He took the child by the hand and said to her, 'Talitha koum,' which means, 'Little girl, I say to you, arise!' The girl, a child of twelve, arose immediately and walked around. [At that] they were utterly astounded. He gave strict orders that no one should know this and said that she should be given something to eat. He departed from there and came to his native place, accompanied by his disciples" (Mark 5:35-43).

When we are faced with tragic circumstances, the attitude that will best serve us is one of trust in God who alone has the power to save.

*"Come, let us return to the Lord, for it is he who has rent, but he will heal us; he has struck us, but He will bind our wounds. He will revive us after two days; on the third day he will raise us up, to live in his presence. Let us know, let us strive to know the Lord; as certain as the dawn is his coming, and his judgment shines forth like the light of day! He will come to us like the rain, like spring rain that waters the earth" (Hosea 6:1-3).*

# CHAPTER IX

## THE HEALING POWER OF JESUS THE LISTENER

### Gratitude to Jesus the Listener in Times of Distress

esus the Listener, when we look at You and think of your suffering, we feel grateful and inspired to thank You for everything You have given us. Now through your grace sustain us during this time of difficulty. Help us accept your will, whatever that may be, with a joyful heart. "When I call, answer me, O my just God, you who relieve me when I am in distress; have pity on me, and hear my prayer!" (Psalm 4:2). We will use all our strength of mind and body to praise You for your precious gift of life. You assumed our human nature in order to redeem us for eternal life. Help us live each day to the full with a spirit of love and humility.

"There was a certain Pharisee who invited Jesus to dine with him. Jesus went to the Pharisee's home and reclined to eat. A woman known in the town to be a sinner learned that he was dining in the Pharisee's home. She brought in a vase of perfumed oil and stood behind him at his feet, weeping so that her tears fell upon his feet. Then she wiped them with her hair, kissing them and perfuming them with the oil. When his host, the Pharisee, saw this, he said to himself, 'If this man were a prophet, he would know who and what sort of woman that is that touches him – that she is a sinner.' In answer to his thoughts, Jesus said to him, 'Simon, I have something to propose to you.' 'Teacher,' he said, 'speak.'

'Two men owed money to a certain money-lender; one owed a total of five hundred coins, the other fifty. Since neither was able to repay, he wrote off both debts. Which of them was more grateful to him?' Simon answered, 'He, I presume, to whom he remitted the larger sum.' Jesus said to him, 'You are right.'

Turning then to the woman, he said to Simon: 'You see this woman? I came to your home and you provided me with no water for my feet. She has washed my feet with her tears and wiped them with her hair. You gave me no kiss, but she has not ceased kissing my feet since I entered. You did not anoint my head with oil, but she has anointed my feet with perfume. I tell you, that is why her many sins are forgiven – because of her great love. Little is forgiven the one whose love is small.'" (Luke 7:36-47).

Not a word was spoken by the woman, not a penny paid. Jesus saw what was in her heart. He acknowledged her attitude of repentance and humility. He restored her worth in the eyes of those who thought her insignificant and who believed they were better than she.

Through the words and actions of Jesus, the woman became aware that Jesus knew her and loved her in spite of her sins. This awareness was the source of her gratitude. Jesus had answered her unspoken longings.

*"Cast your care upon the Lord, and he will support you; never will he permit the just man to be disturbed" (Psalm 55:23).*

## Your Presence, O Jesus the Listener, Gives Us Confidence

our presence in us, O Jesus the Listener, is the source of all our confidence. You are the source of all healing. You are all powerful. We know You love us because You surrendered yourself to the cross so that we might one day have eternal life. Help us when the Evil One tempts us to think otherwise. When we feel physical and emotional pain, we will resist thinking that our struggle is useless. We know You are with us and that we share in your passion. We do not want to feel lonely even when it is difficult to find anyone to help us. We realize that it is always the right time to approach You for what we need and that You are always willing to receive us. You protect us, and so we now place ourselves in your care. We are confident that You are always present in all the circumstances of life. "God is our refuge and our strength, an ever-present help in distress" (Psalm 46:2).

"Later, on the occasion of a Jewish feast, Jesus went up to Jerusalem. Now in Jerusalem by the Sheep Pool there is a place with the Hebrew name Bethesda. Its five porticoes were crowded with sick people lying there blind, lame or disabled [waiting for the movement of the water]. There was one man who had been sick for thirty-eight years. Jesus, who knew he had been sick a long time, said when he saw him lying there, 'Do you want to be healed?' 'Sir,' the sick man answered, 'I do not have anyone to plunge me into the pool once the water has been stirred up. By the time I get there, someone else has gone in ahead of me.' Jesus said to him, 'Stand up! Pick up your mat and walk!' The man was immediately cured; he picked up his mat and began to walk" (John 5:1-9).

hat attracted Jesus to this man? And even more important, what made Jesus respond to the man's needs? The man's patient attitude and his confident trust for thirty-eight years attracted Jesus to him. The man had prayed and hoped to be able to reach the water for so long. Jesus answered him by revealing the truth that He was the life-giving water.

*"O Lord, you have probed me and you know me; you know when I sit and when I stand; you understand my thoughts from afar. My journeys and my rest you scrutinize, with all my ways you are familiar" (Psalm 139:1-3).*

## Lift Our Spirit, O Jesus the Listener, for We Trust in You

ift us in your arms and hold us, O Jesus the Listener, so that we may rest patiently and quietly. Heal us so that we may return to our duties, if that be your holy will. Lift our spirit and give us your peace. "Only in God is my soul at rest; from him comes my salvation. He only is my rock and my salvation, my stronghold; I shall not be disturbed at all" (Psalm 62:2-3). Lord, when we become aware of your love and concern for us, our burdens are made lighter and our confidence in You becomes stronger. Lift us to know your peace and help us trust your love.

"When Mary came to the place where Jesus was, seeing him, she fell at his feet and said to him, 'Lord, if you had been here my brother would never have died.' When Jesus saw her weeping, and the Jews who had accompanied her also weeping, he was troubled in spirit, moved by the deepest emotions. 'Where have you laid him?' he asked. 'Lord, come and see,' they said. Jesus began to weep, which caused the Jews to remark, 'See how much he loved him!' But some said, 'He opened the eyes of that blind man. Why could he not have done something to stop this man from dying?' Once again troubled in spirit, Jesus approached the tomb. It was a cave with a stone laid across it. 'Take away the stone,' Jesus directed. Martha, the dead man's sister, said to him, 'Lord, it has been four days now; surely there will be a stench!'

Jesus replied, 'Did I not assure you that if you believed you would see the glory of God displayed?' They then took away the stone and Jesus looked upward and said: 'Father, I thank you for having heard me. I know that you always hear me but I have said this for the sake of the crowd, that they may believe that you sent me.' Having said this he called loudly, 'Lazarus, come out!' The dead man came out, bound hand and foot with linen strips, his face wrapped in a cloth. 'Untie him,' Jesus told them, 'and let him go free'" (John 11:32-36).

esus was very much affected not only by the death of his friend Lazarus, but also by the trust that Martha and Mary placed in him. This family in Bethany was always present to Jesus and his apostles on their missionary journeys. Jesus now lifts the spirits of those around him with his loving presence in their time of grief. Our consolation is that in spite of all our mistakes, Jesus always remains faithfully present and generously responds to all the good we have ever done.

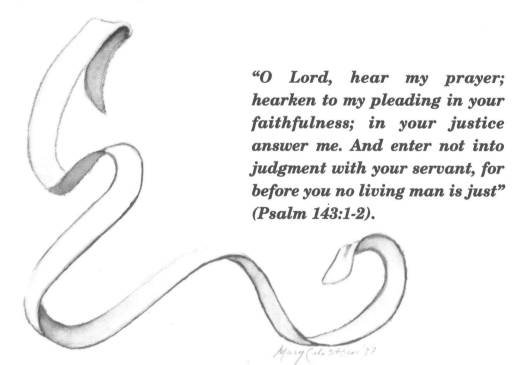

*"O Lord, hear my prayer; hearken to my pleading in your faithfulness; in your justice answer me. And enter not into judgment with your servant, for before you no living man is just"* *(Psalm 143:1-2).*

## Jesus the Listener, Grant Us Mercy

ike the prodigal son who returned to his father's home when he had wasted his inheritance, welcome us, O Jesus the Listener, with peace and mercy at the foot of your cross. We do not ask You for justice for we have sinned and deserve to be judged. We confidently hope for your kindness and forgiveness because we know You love us unconditionally. You embrace us in spite of our guilt. Humbly is the way we come to You today. Hear our cry to You, O Jesus the Listener. We need to share in your peace and experience the warmth of your love. "For you, O Lord, are good and forgiving, abounding in kindness to all who call upon you" (Psalm 86:5).

"They came to Jericho next, and as he was leaving that place with his disciples and a sizable crowd, there was a blind beggar Bartimaeus ('son of Timaeus') sitting by the roadside. On hearing that it was Jesus of Nazareth, he began to call out, 'Jesus, Son of David, have pity on me!' Many people were scolding him to make him keep quiet, but he shouted all the louder, 'Son of David, have pity on me!' Then Jesus stopped and said, 'Call him over.' So they called the blind man over, telling him as they did so, 'You have nothing to fear from him! Get up! He is calling you!' He threw aside his cloak, jumped up and came to Jesus. Jesus asked him, 'What do you want me to do for you?' 'Rabboni,' the blind man said, 'I want to see.' Jesus said in reply, 'Be on your way! Your faith has healed you.' Immediately he received his sight and started to follow him up the road" (Mark 10:46-52).

here was no embarrassment, no shame, no fear, no abusive reaction from the crowd that would keep Bartimaeus from publicly declaring his need and professing his faith in Jesus. Bartimaeus trusted that Jesus would listen. He seized the opportunity to declare Jesus of Nazareth the Son of David. He asked for mercy. When Bartimaeus heard that Jesus was passing by, he knew through faith that no one Jesus touched would remain the same. Because Bartimaeus was able to recognize Jesus as the promised and long-awaited Messiah, Jesus granted him human sight to behold his personal Savior.

*"When I behold your heavens, the work of your fingers, the moon and the stars which you set in place – What is man that you should be mindful of him, or the son of man that you should care for him? You have made him little less than the angels, and crowned him with glory and honor" (Psalm 8:4-6).*

## Jesus the Listener, the Divine Physician

Jesus the Listener, place your hands upon us and make us whole. Even now, we know your grace is healing us and giving us strength. We surrender ourselves to your guidance and protection. Make us an example to others of your healing grace as we acknowledge your blessings upon us in spite of our offenses and omissions. "Incline your ear, O Lord; answer me, for I am afflicted and poor. Keep my life, for I am devoted to you; save your servant who trusts in you. You are my God; have pity on me, O Lord, for to you I call all the day" (Psalm 86:2-3).

"As he moved on, Jesus saw a man named Matthew at his post where taxes were collected. He said to him, 'Follow me.' Matthew got up and followed him. Now it happened that, while Jesus was at table in Matthew's home, many tax collectors and those known as sinners came to join Jesus and his disciples at dinner. The Pharisees saw this and complained to his disciples, 'What reason can the Teacher have for eating with tax collectors and those who disregard the law?' Overhearing the remark, he said: 'People who are in good health do not need a doctor; sick people do. Go and learn the meaning of the words, 'It is mercy I desire and not sacrifice.' I have come to call, not the self-righteous, but sinners'" (Matthew 9:9-13).

he prescription of God for eternal life is "Keep my commands and live" (Proverbs 7:2). The most important of the commandments is to love God and to love our neighbor. When Jesus was asked who our neighbor is, He told the parable of the Good Samaritan in which our neighbor is the person in need closest to us (cf. Luke 10:25-37). The true love of neighbor has to be based on a sincere desire to do good for its own sake and not simply to fulfill a requirement of the law. This teaching of Jesus may likely lead to difficulties because in following the example of the Divine Physician, we might be called upon to live in a manner that might be considered to be socially unacceptable, economically unprofitable, and politically incorrect.

*"Though I am afflicted and poor, yet the Lord thinks of me. You are my help and my deliverer; O my God, hold not back!" (Psalm 40:18).*

# CHAPTER X

## TOGETHER IN PRAYER

### Prayer for People Who Serve Others

hank You, O Jesus the Listener, for those who wish to see the physical and spiritual health of others improve. Grant physicians insight. Steady the hands of surgeons. Give nurses, technicians, and all medical staffs counsel and patience, and bless their enthusiasm for self-sacrifice. O Jesus the Listener, inspire chaplains with words of healing and comfort. Bless all the administrative, clerical, and supportive personnel that keep hospitals running smoothly. Bless all researchers with great success over incurable diseases. Comfort everyone in the face of death. May we all realize that in helping others, we are really helping You. Make us humble in acknowledging that "our help is in the name of the Lord, who made heaven and earth" (Psalm 123:8).

"At Lystra there was a man who was lame from birth; he used to sit crippled, never having walked in his life. On one occasion he was listening to Paul preaching, and Paul looked directly at him and saw that he had the faith to be saved. He called out to him in a loud voice, 'Stand up! On your feet!' The man jumped up and began to walk around. When the crowds saw what Paul had done, they cried out in Lycaonian, 'Gods have come to us in the form of men!' They named Barnabas Zeus; Paul they called Hermes, since he was the spokesman. Even the priest of the temple of Zeus, which stood outside the town, brought oxen and garlands to the gates because he wished to offer sacrifice to them with the crowds.

When the apostles Barnabas and Paul heard of this, they tore their garments and rushed out into the crowd. 'Friends, why do you do this?' they shouted frantically. 'We are only men, human like you. We are bringing you the good news that will convert you from just such follies as these to the living God, 'the one who made heaven and earth and the sea and all that is in them.' In past ages he let the Gentiles go their way. Yet in bestowing his benefits, he has not hidden himself completely, without a clue. From the heavens he sends down rain and rich harvests; your spirits he fills with food and delight'" (Acts 14:8-17).

God is the author of life. He calls upon men and women to intervene on his behalf in order to serve, protect and save life. At the Last Judgment, God will judge us according to how well we have carried out this responsibility. "Come. You have my Father's blessing! Inherit the kingdom prepared for you from the creation of the world. For I was hungry and you gave me food, I was thirsty and you gave me drink. I was a stranger and you welcomed me, naked and you clothed me. I was ill and you comforted me, in prison and you came to visit me" (Matthew 25:34-36).

Our response to this divine sharing of talents and resources in the service of others should always be gratitude and the acknowledgment that God, and He alone, is the Lord of life.

*"I am the good shepherd. A good shepherd lays down his life for the sheep. A hired man, who is not a shepherd and whose sheep are not his own, sees a wolf coming and leaves the sheep and runs away, and the wolf catches and scatters them. This is because he works for pay and has no concern for the sheep. I am the good shepherd, and I know mine and mine know me, just as the Father knows me and I know the Father; and I will lay down my life for the sheep" (John 10:11-15).*

## Prayer for Young People

Jesus the Listener, You love young people and the innocence they possess. You showed your love by curing them whenever they were brought to You. Restore them to health of mind and body. Spare all young people, O Jesus the Listener, so that they may serve You in the future. We call upon their guardian angels in heaven who constantly behold the face of God to protect them. O Jesus the Listener, stretch out your hands and touch all young people who are ill. "Children too are a gift from the Lord, the fruit of the womb, a reward. Like arrows in the hand of a warrior are the children born in one's youth. Blessed are they whose quivers are full" (Psalm 127:3-5).

"'Teacher,' a man in the crowd replied, 'I have brought my son to you because he is possessed by a mute spirit. Whenever it seizes him it throws him down; he foams at the mouth and grinds his teeth and becomes rigid. Just now I asked your disciples to expel him, but they were unable to do so. He replied by saying to the crowd, 'What an unbelieving lot you are! How long must I remain with you? How long can I endure you? Bring him to me.' When they did so the spirit caught sight of Jesus and immediately threw the boy into convulsions. As he fell to the ground he began to roll around and foam at the mouth. Then Jesus questioned the father: 'How long has this been happening to him?' 'From childhood,' the father replied. 'Often it throws him into fire and into water. You would think it would kill him. If out of the kindness of your heart you can do anything to help us, please do!' Jesus said,

'If you can? Everything is possible to a man who trusts.' The boy's father immediately exclaimed, 'I do believe! Help my lack of trust!' Jesus, on seeing a crowd rapidly gather, reprimanded the unclean spirit by saying to him, 'Mute and deaf spirit, I command you: Get out of him and never enter him again!' Shouting, and throwing the boy into convulsions, it came out of him; the boy became like a corpse, which caused many to say, 'He is dead.' But Jesus took him by the hand and helped him to his feet. When Jesus arrived at the house his disciples began to ask him privately, 'Why is it that we could not expel it?' He told them, 'This kind you can drive out only by prayer'" (Mark 9:14-29).

The Evil One always looks to overcome and destroy what God has made beautiful and good. Particularly hideous is any evil or violence done to the innocent, especially young people. Jesus tells us that "it would be better for anyone who leads astray one of these little ones who believe in me, to be drowned by a millstone around his neck, in the depths of the sea" (Matthew 18:6). While Jesus is the only one who can save us from the power of the Evil One, we must do all we can to fortify ourselves with prayer, and also to take responsibility to help others from becoming victims of evil, especially young people, by our constant vigilance and care.

*"Then children were brought to him that he might lay his hands on them and pray. The disciples rebuked them, but Jesus said, 'Let the children come to me, and do not prevent them; for the kingdom of heaven belongs to such as these'" (Matthew 19:13-14).*

## Prayer for All in Emotional Difficulty

 Jesus the Listener, give peace to all who experience a troubled mind and who are not able to communicate well with You. Have mercy and restore the health of all who live in emotional suffering and loneliness. Expel unwholesome thoughts that torment and lead to discouragement. Help us believe that You protect us from harm and that You died out of love for us. Bring comfort and peace to our families. Provide understanding people and whatever else is necessary to help all in distress experience fulfilling lives. "The Lord is faithful in all his words and holy in all his works. The Lord lifts up all who are falling and raises up all who are bowed down. The eyes of all look hopefully to you, and you give them their food in due season; you open your hand and satisfy the desire of every living thing" (Psalm 145:14-16).

"From that place he went off to the territory of Tyre and Sidon. He retired to a certain house and wanted no one to recognize him; however, he could not escape notice. Soon a woman, whose small daughter had an unclean spirit, heard about him. She approached him and crouched at his feet. The woman who was Greek – a Syro-Phoenician by birth – began to beg him to expel the demon from her daughter. He told her: 'Let the sons of the household satisfy themselves at table first. It is not right to take the food of the children and throw it to the dogs.' 'Please, Lord,' she replied, 'even the dogs under the table eat the family's leavings.' Then he said to her, 'For such a reply, be off now! The demon has already left your daughter.' When she got home, she found the child lying in bed and the demon gone" (Mark 7:24-30).

ne may tend to believe that the miracles of Jesus are meant only for a few chosen people. There could be nothing further from the truth. In fact, Jesus has a preferential love for those who suffer. Therefore, we must be bold in our resolve to keep asking for the fulfillment of our needs and not be distracted or discouraged by what seems to be denial or rejection. It is good for us to pray for the wisdom to recognize God's goodness in all things, especially when we find it difficult to understand and appreciate his ways, and his timing.

*"When I say, 'My foot is slipping,' your kindness, O Lord, sustains me; when cares abound within me, your comfort gladdens my soul"* *(Psalm 95:18-19).*

## Prayer for Self-Knowledge

Jesus the Listener, may we never forget that our heavenly Father made each of us a masterpiece of his creation, unique and irreplaceable, and one of a kind. He created us in his image, and You redeemed us so that we would know the joys of eternal life. Help us to remember these truths so that in difficult moments we may not lose sight of our true identity. We ask You to make us the recipients of your grace so that we may discover our God-given talents and gifts. May we use them constructively to serve You and to love others as we love ourselves. Being the children of God, we pray that one day we may be able to say with the Apostle Paul: "I have fought the good fight, I have finished the race, I have kept the faith. From now on a merited crown awaits me; on that Day the Lord, just judge that he is, will award it to me – and not only to me, but to all who have looked for his appearing with eager longing" (2 Timothy 4:6-8).

"On a sabbath day he was teaching in one of the synagogues. There was a woman there who for eighteen years had been possessed by a spirit which drained her strength. She was badly stooped – quite incapable of standing erect. When Jesus saw her, he called her to him, and said, 'Woman, you are free of your infirmity.' He laid his hand on her, and immediately she stood up straight and began thanking God" (Luke 13:11-13).

here is always the possibility that we may face many varied and difficult situations in life that make us "badly stooped – quite incapable of standing erect." Knowing that we are the children of God enables us to remember that our lives are dependent on a loving and provident Father. "Which one of you would hand his son a stone when he asks for a loaf of bread, or a snake when he asks for a fish? If you then, who are wicked, know how to give good gifts to your children, how much more will your heavenly Father give good things to those who ask him" (Matthew. 7:9-11).

*"Blessed are you in the firmament of heaven, praiseworthy and glorious forever. Stars of heaven, bless the Lord; praise and exalt him above all forever. Servants of the Lord, bless the Lord; praise and exalt him above all forever. Holy men of humble heart, bless the Lord; praise and exalt him above all forever"* (Daniel 3:56,63,85,87).

## Prayer to Overcome Anxiety

esus the Listener, we are full of apprehension and not able to free ourselves from anxiety. You told us: "Your heavenly Father knows all that you need. Seek first his kingship over you, his way of holiness, and all these things will be given you besides" (Matthew 7:32-33). Grant us the grace to trust and hope in You and not rely on our own strength alone. "A king is not saved by a mighty army, nor is a warrior delivered by great strength. Useless is the horse for safety; great though its strength, it cannot provide escape. But see, the eyes of the Lord are upon those who fear him, upon those who hope for his kindness, to deliver them from death and preserve them in spite of famine" (Psalm 33:16-19).

"As Jesus entered Capernaum, a centurion approached him with this request: 'Sir, my serving boy is at home in bed paralyzed, suffering painfully.' He said to him, 'I will come and cure him.' 'Sir,' the centurion said in reply, 'I am not worthy to have you under my roof. Just give an order and my boy will get better. I am a man under authority myself and I have troops assigned to me. If I give one man the order, 'Dismissed,' off he goes. If I say to another, 'Come here,' he comes. If I tell my slave, 'Do this,' he does it.' Jesus showed amazement on hearing this and remarked to his followers, 'I assure you, I have never found this much faith in Israel'" (Matthew 8:3-7).

41

veryone receives enough faith to believe and to trust in the providence of God. While not of the Jewish faith, the centurion was able to recognize in Jesus someone close to God who could act with authority. The centurion's faith was based on his personal experience of authority, and on the power that Jesus always manifested in the presence of illness. The centurion trusted that Jesus could and would exercise this power in the cure of the paralyzed boy. Jesus praised the centurion's faith and rewarded his trust.

*"My strength and my courage is the Lord, and he has been my savior"* (Psalm 118:14).

## Prayer before a Surgical Procedure

 Jesus the Listener, your healing presence is needed now more than ever. Your love dispels fear and anxiety in the midst of uncertainty. You are the Savior of the world, and we have nothing to fear. With St. Peter, we confess our faith: "Lord, to whom shall we go? You have the words of eternal life… We are convinced that you are God's holy one" (John 6:68-69). Give us life, O Jesus the Listener, that we may continue to praise and adore You. Forgive the foolish mistakes of our youth, and all the words and deeds of our lives that did not include You. Allow us to return to our loved ones in good health proclaiming your compassion "for you have dominion over life and death" (Wisdom 16:13).

"Soon afterward he went to a town called Naim, and his disciples and a large crowd accompanied him. As he approached the gate of the town a dead man was being carried out, the only son of a widowed mother. A considerable crowd of townsfolk were with her. The Lord was moved with pity upon seeing her and said to her, 'Do not cry.' Then he stepped forward and touched the litter; at this, the bearers halted. He said, 'Young man, I bid you get up.' The dead man sat up and began to speak. Then Jesus gave him back to his mother" (Luke 7:11-15).

ur lives are a sequence of events that alter the way we think and behave. They are always grace-filled opportunities for spiritual growth because God is active in them all. We are not able to be totally aware of all that God is doing in our lives. The widow of Naim was so consumed with sorrow over the death of her only son, and with the uncertainty of her future life, that she was understandably not aware of the presence of Jesus. But He was there for her. As the custodian of life, Jesus is forever taking the initiative to bring forth joy from sorrow, hope from despair, and life from death.

*"Sing to the Lord a new song; sing to the Lord, all you lands. Sing to the Lord, bless his name; announce his salvation, day after day. Tell his glory among the nations; among all peoples, his wondrous deeds" (Psalm 96:1-3).*

## Prayer after a Surgical Procedure

Jesus the Listener, in the midst of all pain and suffering, we want to recall the words of the Prophet Isaiah: "Fear not, for I have redeemed you; I have called you by name: you are mine" (Isaiah 43:1). Thank You for having preserved your gift of life in us. We want to occupy this time of recuperation in loving and praising You, and in bearing witness to others of your providential care. In union with your passion and death, we offer all discomfort for the remission of our sins and those of others. Grant us the gift of rest so that we may regain our strength. In silence, may we find your healing. "Sing to the Lord with thanksgiving; with the lyre celebrate our God who covers the heavens with clouds, provides rain for the earth, makes grass sprout on the mountains, who gives animals their food and ravens what they cry for...The Lord takes pleasure in the devout, those who await his faithful care" (Psalm 147:8-11).

"On his journey to Jerusalem he passed along the borders of Samaria and Galilee. As he was entering a village, ten lepers met him. Keeping their distance, they raised their voices and said, 'Jesus, Master, have pity on us!' When he saw them, he responded, 'Go and show yourselves to the priests.' On their way there they were cured. One of them, realizing that he had been cured, came back praising God in a loud voice. He threw himself on his face at the feet of Jesus and spoke his praises. This man was a Samaritan.

Jesus took the occasion to say, 'Were not all ten made whole? Where are the other nine? Was there no one to return and give thanks to God except this foreigner?' He said to the man, 'Stand up and go your way; your faith has been your salvation'" (Luke 17:11-19).

hen a crisis is over, or a need has been fulfilled, it is so easy to forget to be grateful. Expressing gratitude for a favor received shows a humble acceptance of the truth that we are not self-sufficient. Every time we thank someone, we overcome pride, we empty ourselves of selfishness, and we acknowledge the grace of God at work in us.

*"O Lord, my God, I cried out to you and you healed me. O Lord, you brought me up from the nether world; you preserved me from among those going down into the pit. Sing praise to the Lord, you his faithful ones, and give thanks to his holy name"* (Psalm 30:3-5).

## Prayer in Times of Loneliness

he Prophet Jonah turned to You O Lord in his loneliness in the belly of the large fish. We also come before You, O Jesus the Listener, and ask You to lift us from our sadness and discouragement as you did for Jonah: "The waters swirled about me, threatening my life; the abyss enveloped me; seaweed clung about my head. Down I went to the roots of the mountains; the bars of the nether world were closing behind me forever. But you brought up my life from the pit, O Lord, my God. When my soul fainted within me, I remembered the Lord; my prayer reached you in your holy temple" (Jonah 2:6-8). At moments of crisis, we may feel weak and vulnerable, and very distant from everyone. Lord, You taught us that You are never separated from us. We ask that You give us the security we need to believe and trust in your love. We also ask You to remember all the lonely of this world. Give them the joy that comes from your peaceful and gentle presence.

"A woman with a hemorrhage of twelve years' duration, incurable at any doctor's hands, came up behind him and touched the tassel on his cloak. Immediately her bleeding stopped. Jesus asked, 'Who touched me?' Everyone disclaimed doing it, while Peter said, 'Lord, the crowds are milling and pressing around you!' Jesus insisted, 'Someone touched me; I know that power has gone forth from me.' When the woman saw that her act had not gone unnoticed, she came forward trembling. Falling at his feet, she related before the whole assemblage why she had touched him and how she had been instantly cured. Jesus said to her, 'Daughter, it is your faith that has cured you. Now go in peace'" (Luke 8:43-48).

oneliness has many causes and many consequences. Most of the causes of loneliness may be beyond our control, for example, environment, prejudice, hatred, illness, mistrust, betrayal, and abuse. The consequences of loneliness may be severe, such as depression, illness, despair, and even suicide. At first sight, it would seem that loneliness is insurmountable. However, from the Scriptures we learn that sincere and persevering prayer offered by a lonely person, as in the cases of Jonah and the woman with the hemorrhage, enables us to focus our attention on the providential and salvific plan of God.

In reflecting upon loneliness, it is beneficial to distinguish it from a solitude chosen for spiritual enrichment. While loneliness may be considered a detrimental psychological state, solitude is usually the result of a free choice for the purpose of personal growth. Loneliness tends to sadden and discourage an individual, while solitude may enlighten and deepen one's power of reflection and understanding. While loneliness tends to deteriorate the spiritual and emotional quality of one's life, solitude chosen for spiritual growth, on the other hand, may be of great benefit to one's well-being.

*"You changed my mourning into dancing; you took off my sackcloth and clothed me with gladness, that my soul might sing praise to you without ceasing; O Lord, my God, forever will I give you thanks" (Psalm 30:12-13).*

# CHAPTER XI

## LIVING IN THE PRESENCE OF GOD

**Morning Meditation**

hank you for this new day, O Jesus the Listener. "When I lie down in sleep, I wake again, for the Lord sustains me" (Psalm 3:6). Thank You for the gift of life which allows us to share in your divine and eternal life. Thank You for the gift of the Holy Spirit who inspires and sanctifies us. We thank You; we adore You; we praise You; we worship You, and we give You glory. Help us to be more compassionate and generous, and love others as You commanded. "Hearken to my words, O Lord, attend to my sighing. Heed my call for help, my king and my God! To you I pray, O Lord; at dawn you hear my voice; at dawn I bring my plea expectantly before you" (Psalm 5:2-3). Let me rejoice with the Psalmist: "This is the day the Lord has made; let us be glad and rejoice in it" (Psalm 118:24).

*Harry Celestino — 1997*

"Jesus then said to his disciples: 'If a man wishes to come after me, he must deny his very self, take up his cross, and begin to follow in my footsteps. Whoever would save his life will lose it, but whoever loses his life for my sake will find it'" (Matthew 17:24-25).

Each new day gives us a chance to make new choices. Even though the ability to make choices affords us a great deal of freedom, it also is a great responsibility. To make decisions that bring about good results for us and others, we need to follow in the footsteps of Jesus.

*"Show me the way in which I should walk, for to you I lift up my soul" (Psalm 143:8).*

50

## Evening Meditation

Thank You, O Jesus the Listener, for all the gifts You shared with us this day through the presence of your Holy Spirit. We thank You for having died on the Cross for our salvation. We thank You also for the maternal care of your Blessed Mother. Allow us to rest in safety during the night for You are our Good Shepherd, and in verdant pastures You give us repose. During the night, we place our lives into your hands. May St. Joseph, your foster father, protect us as he protected You. We thank You, O Jesus, for having given us a guardian angel whom You entrusted with our care. O Jesus the Listener, let your Precious Blood cleanse us of all our sins. Bring us safely through the night so that we may again adore You in the morning.

> "We are afflicted in every way possible, but we are not crushed; full of doubts, we never despair. We are persecuted but never abandoned; we are struck down but never destroyed. Continually we carry about in our bodies the dying of Jesus, so that in our bodies the life of Jesus may also be revealed" (2 Corinthians 4:8-10).

Through the Holy Spirit, we are able to witness God's revelation of love in the suffering of Jesus and believe in the promise of eternal reward that it contains. Although we will experience unhappiness in the course of our earthly life, we can successfully use our suffering for individual and communal redemption. There will be events in our lives that cause unrest, stress, and anxiety. But the way Jesus faced suffering in his own life inspires us to endure ours with the same self-sacrificial love. By offering our suffering to the Father in union with the suffering of Jesus, we have the certainty of sharing in his peace and victorious resurrection.

*"Let my prayer come like incense before you; the lifting up of my hands, like the evening sacrifice" (Psalm 141:2).*

51

## O Guardian Angel, Constant Companion of Our Life

 Guardian Angel, we are so important in the eyes of the Lord that He has appointed you to be our special companion for life. We thank you for all the times that you protected and saved us from harm, even without our awareness. You safeguard us from evil with all the power that the Lord has given you. How glorious it is that you behold the Beatific Vision. One day you will usher our souls before the Lord, and we hope to share the same Vision. Keep our eyes fixed on Paradise so that at the appointed time we may safely return home to our Creator. Like the Psalmist, we will remember the Lord's graciousness in appointing you to accompany us on our journey. "Because you have the Lord for your refuge; you have made the Most High your stronghold. No evil shall befall you, nor shall affliction come near your tent, for to his angels he has given command about you, that they guard you in all your ways" (Psalm 91:9-11).

> "The Son of Man will dispatch his angels to collect from his kingdom all who draw others to apostasy, and all evildoers. The angels will hurl them into the fiery furnace where they will wail and grind their teeth. Then the saints will shine like the sun in their Father's kingdom. Let everyone heed what he hears!" (Matthew 13:41-42).

Angels were present at the beginning of creation, and they will be present on the day of judgment. They are intelligent spirits who have been appointed by God to serve Him and us by announcing his saving plan. What a comforting thought that from our infancy until the last day of our life, we have the very powerful help of a Guardian Angel from whom we can seek help in good times and in bad.

*"Bless the Lord, all you his angels, you mighty in strength, who do his bidding, obeying his spoken word" (Psalm 103:20).*

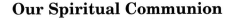

## Our Spiritual Communion

 Jesus the Listener, You assumed a human body out of love for us, and that same body suffered on a cross on our behalf. We were washed clean by your Blood. Through your words and actions at the Last Supper, You remain miraculously with us. "'Take this and eat it,' he said, 'this is my body.' Then he took a cup, gave thanks, and gave it to them. 'All of you must drink from it,' he said, 'for this is my blood, the blood of the covenant, to be poured out in behalf of many for the forgiveness of sins'" (Matthew 26:26-28). We thank You for the privilege You bestowed on us at our First Holy Communion, and we always hope to grow in gratitude. O Jesus the Listener, since we are not able to receive You sacramentally at this time, we desire to receive You spiritually. Your body is the bread of life; your words, our sustenance. Allow us to experience your Eucharistic presence through this Spiritual Communion until the Beatific Vision of Paradise.

*"As the hind longs for the running waters, so my soul longs for you, O God. Athirst is my soul for God, the living God. When shall I go and behold the face of God?" (Psalm 42:2-3).*

53

"Jesus called his disciples to him and said: 'My heart is moved with pity for the crowd. By now they have been with me three days, and have nothing to eat. I do not wish to send them away hungry, for fear they may collapse on the way. His disciples said to him, 'How could we ever get enough bread in this deserted spot to satisfy such a crowd?' But Jesus asked them, 'How many loaves of bread do you have?' 'Seven,' they replied, 'and a few small fish.' Then he directed the crowd to seat themselves on the ground. He took the seven loaves and the fish, and after giving thanks he broke them and gave them to the disciples, who in turn gave them to the crowds. All ate until they were full. When they gathered up the fragments left over, these filled seven hampers. The people who were fed numbered four thousand, apart from women and children" (Matthew 15:32).

*"I myself am the bread of life. No one who comes to me shall ever be hungry, no one who believes in me shall ever thirst" (John 6:35).*

## Daily Prayer of Gratitude

Jesus the Listener, You taught us how to pray and that it is proper for us to ask our Father to "give us today our daily bread" (Matthew 6:11). We thank You for all your gifts and praise You for your goodness to us. We pray particularly for the poor. We ask your blessings upon all of us in due season. "You open your hand and satisfy the desire of every living thing" (Psalm 145:16).

*"Look at the birds in the sky. They do not sow or reap, they gather nothing into barns; yet your heavenly Father feeds them. Are not you more important than they? Which of you by worrying can add a moment to his life-span?...Your heavenly Father knows all that you need" (Matthew 6:26-27;32).*

# CHAPTER XII

## OUR LADY'S CREED

### St. Gabriel of Our Lady of Sorrows, Passionist Saint

 believe, O Mary, that you are the mother of all. I believe that you are our life and, after God, the sole refuge of sinners.

I believe that you are the strength of Christians, and their help, especially at the hour of death; that following you, I shall not stray; that praying to you, I shall not be abandoned; that standing with you, I shall not fall.

I believe that you are ready to aid those who call upon you, that you are the salvation of those who invoke you, and that you are willing to do more good for us than we can desire; that even when not asked, you do hasten to our assistance.

I believe that in your name is to be found a sweetness like that experienced by St. Bernard of Clairvaux in the name of Jesus – that it is joy to the heart, honey to the mouth and music to the ears and that, after the name of Jesus, there is no other name through which the faithful receive so much grace, so much hope and so much consolation.

I believe that you are a Co-Redemptrix with Christ for our salvation, that all the graces which God dispenses pass through your hands, and that no one will enter heaven except through you who are rightly called the "Gate of Heaven."

believe that true devotion to you is a most certain sign of eternal salvation. I believe that you are superior to all the saints and angels, and that God alone surpasses you.

I believe that God has given you in the highest possible degree, all the graces, special and general, with which He can favor humankind.

I believe that your beauty and excellence surpass that of all angels and all people.

I believe that you alone do fulfill perfectly the precept: "You shall love the Lord your God" and that the very Seraphim of heaven can learn from your heart how to love God.

I believe that if all the love which all mothers have for their children, all that husbands and wives have for each other, all that all the angels and saints have for those who are devoted to them, were united in one, it would not equal the love that you have for even one soul.

*"'Woman, there is your son.' In turn he said to the disciple, 'There is your mother.' From that hour onward, the disciple took her into his care"* *(John 19:27).*

# CHAPTER XIII

## TREASURY OF PRAYERS

### The Sign of the Cross

In the Name of the Father and of the Son and of the Holy Spirit. Amen.

> The Sign of the Cross expresses our Christian belief in the greatest mysteries of our faith: the mystery of the Blessed Trinity, the Incarnation, and Redemption. The words we say in the Sign of the Cross show that God is one in three Divine Persons. The Sign of the Cross reminds us that Jesus Christ, the Son of God, saved us through his sacrifice on the cross.

### Glory to the Father

Glory to the Father, and to the Son, and to the Holy Spirit. As it was in the beginning, is now, and will be for ever. Amen.

### Our Father

Our Father, who art in heaven, hallowed be thy name; thy kingdom come; thy will be done on earth, as it is in heaven. Give us this day our daily bread; and forgive us our trespasses, as we forgive those who trespass against us; and lead us not into temptation, but deliver us from evil. Amen.

**Hail Mary**

Hail Mary, full of grace, the Lord is with you; blessed are you among women, and blessed is the fruit of your womb, Jesus. Holy Mary, Mother of God, pray for us sinners, now and at the hour of our death. Amen.

**Eternal Rest**

Eternal rest grant unto them, O Lord, and let perpetual light shine upon them. May they rest in peace. Amen.

**Hail, Holy Queen**

Hail, holy Queen, Mother of Mercy, our life, our sweetness and our hope! To you do we cry, poor banished children of Eve. To you do we send up our sighs, mourning and weeping in this valley of tears. Turn then, most gracious Advocate, your eyes of mercy toward us. And after this our exile show unto us the blessed fruit of your womb, Jesus. O clement, O loving, O sweet Virgin Mary.

**Prayer to St. Joseph**

O Blessed St. Joseph, we honor you as the most watchful guardian of the Holy Family and faithful spouse of Mary the Mother of God. It was your privilege to diligently protect Jesus and Mary while they were under your care on earth. With confidence in your powerful intercession before the throne of God, we ask you to obtain our requests. *(In silence mention your requests.)* Protect us, our families and friends from all spiritual and physical harm. Teach us your virtues of humility, obedience, prudence and patience. Help us to be pure in our thoughts, words, and actions. Assist us to fulfill with joy the duties and responsibilities of our states in life. Be our constant guide in our daily activities so that we may be called "upright" before God as you were (cf. Matthew 1:19). Strengthened by your example, may we live holy lives so that we may die as you did in the arms of Jesus and Mary.

*The Authors*

61

**Prayer to St. Michael the Archangel**

Saint Michael the Archangel, defend us in battle; be our defense against the wickedness and snares of the devil. May God rebuke him, we humbly pray; and do you, O Prince of the heavenly host, by the power of God, thrust into hell Satan and the other evil spirits who prowl about the world seeking the ruin of souls. Amen.

**Prayer to Our Guardian Angel**

Angel of God, my guardian dear, to whom God's love entrusts me here, ever this day be at my side, to light and guard, to rule and guide.

**Morning Prayer**

O Jesus, through the Immaculate Heart of Mary, I offer You my prayers, works, joys and sufferings of this day in union with the Holy Sacrifice of the Mass throughout the world. I offer them for all the intentions of your Sacred Heart: the salvation of souls, reparation for sin, the reunion of all Christians. I offer them for the intentions of our Bishops and of all our associates, and in particular for those recommended by our Holy Father this month. Amen.

**Evening Prayer**

O my God, I adore You, and I love You with all my heart. I thank You for having created me and saved me by your grace, and for having preserved me during this day. I pray that You will take for yourself whatever good I might have done this day, and that You will forgive me whatever evil I have done. Protect me this night, and may your grace be with me always. Amen.

## Act of Contrition

O my God, I am heartily sorry for having offended You, and I detest all my sins, because I dread the loss of heaven and the pains of hell, but most of all because they offend You, my God, who are all-good and deserving of all my love. I firmly resolve, with the help of your grace, to confess my sins, to do penance, and to amend my life. Amen.

## Act of Faith

O my God, I firmly believe that You are one God in three Divine Persons, the Father, the Son, and the Holy Spirit. I believe in Jesus Christ, your Son, who became man and died for our sins, and who will come to judge the living and the dead. I believe these and all the truths which the Holy Catholic Church teaches, because You have revealed them, who can neither deceive nor be deceived. Amen.

## Act of Hope

O my God, trusting in your infinite goodness and promises, I hope to obtain pardon of my sins, the help of your grace, and life everlasting, through the merits of Jesus Christ, my Lord and Redeemer. Amen.

## Act of Love

O my God, I love You above all things, with my whole heart and soul, because You are all-good and worthy of all my love. I love my neighbor as myself for love of You. I forgive all who have injured me, and I ask pardon of all whom I have injured. Amen.

## Grace before Meals

Bless us, O Lord, and these your gifts, which we are about to receive from your bounty, through Christ Our Lord. Amen.

## Grace after Meals

We give You thanks for all your benefits, O Almighty God, who lives and reigns forever. May the souls of the faithful departed through the mercy of God, rest in peace. Amen.

**The Divine Praises (in Reparation of Sins)**

Blessed be God.

Blessed be his holy Name.

Blessed be Jesus Christ, true God and true Man.

Blessed be the name of Jesus.

Blessed be his Most Sacred Heart.

Blessed be his Most Precious Blood.

Blessed be Jesus in the Most Holy Sacrament of the Altar.

Blessed be the Holy Spirit, the Paraclete.

Blessed be the great Mother of God, Mary most holy.

Blessed be her holy and Immaculate Conception.

Blessed be her glorious Assumption.

Blessed be the name of Mary, Virgin and Mother.

Blessed be St. Joseph, her most chaste Spouse.

Blessed be God in his angels and in his saints.

## The Apostles' Creed
## (Profession of Faith)

I believe in God, the Father Almighty, Creator of heaven and earth. I believe in Jesus Christ, his only Son, our Lord. He was conceived by the power of the Holy Spirit and born of the Virgin Mary. He suffered under Pontius Pilate, was crucified, died, and was buried. He descended to the dead. On the third day He rose again. He ascended into heaven, and is seated at the right hand of the Father. He will come again to judge the living and the dead. I believe in the Holy Spirit, the Holy Catholic Church, the communion of saints, the forgiveness of sins, the resurrection of the body, and the life everlasting. Amen.

**Prayer to Jesus Crucified**

Lord Jesus, how many ages have You hung upon your cross, and still I pass You by and regard You not, except to pierce anew your Sacred Heart? How often have I passed You by, heedless of your great sorrow, your many wounds, your infinite Love? How often have I stood before You, not to comfort and console You, but to add to your sorrows, to deepen your wounds, to scorn your Love? You have stretched forth your hands to comfort me, to raise me up, and I have taken those hands that might have struck me into hell, and bent them back on the cross, and nailed them there, rigid and helpless. Yet, I have but succeeded in engraving my name on your palms forever. You have loved me with an infinite Love, and I have taken advantage of that Love to sin the more against You. Yet, my ingratitude has but pierced your Sacred Heart, and upon me has flowed your Precious Blood. Lord Jesus, let your blood be upon me, not for a curse, but for a blessing. Lamb of God, You take away the sins of the world. Have mercy on me. Amen.

**The Memorare**

Remember, O most gracious Virgin Mary, that never was it known that anyone who fled to your protection, implored your help or sought your intercession, was left unaided. Inspired with this confidence, I fly to you, O Virgin of virgins, my Mother. To you I come; before you I stand, sinful and sorrowful. O Mother of the Word Incarnate! Despise not my petitions, but in your mercy hear and answer me. Amen.

## Prayer to Our Mother of Sorrows

O Sorrowful Mother, through Divine Grace you always had the courage to do God's holy will, especially in moments of trial.

At the foot of the Cross, you accepted your personal agony as you watched your Son sacrifice his life for our salvation. You gave us an example to emulate whenever we are called upon to endure suffering.

You are the new Eve, the Woman who shared in restoring the life of Grace that was lost through original sin. You always lead us back to Jesus whenever we stray.

As the faithful handmaid of the Lord, we ask you to intercede for us before the throne of God, so that in our sorrow and distress, we may know his peace and love. As our loving Mother, let your maternal arms embrace us and keep us safe from all harm.

At the end of our earthly life, pray for us so that Jesus your Son will take us home to the Father. Shelter us under your mantle so that we may receive mercy and forgiveness for our sins and be numbered among the blessed. Amen.

*The Authors*

## The Fatima Prayer

O my Jesus, forgive us our sins, save us from the fire of hell, take all souls to heaven, and help especially those most in need of your mercy.

## Anima Christi

Soul of Christ, sanctify me.

Body of Christ, save me.

Blood of Christ, inebriate me.

Water from the side of Christ, wash me.

Passion of Christ, strengthen me.

O good Jesus, hear me.

Within your wounds hide me.

Separated from you let me never be.

From the malignant enemy, defend me.

At the hour of death, call me.

And close to You bid me.

That with your saints I may be

Praising You, for all eternity. Amen.

*"May the Passion of Our Lord Jesus Christ and the sorrows of Mary our Blessed Mother be ever in our hearts" (Passionist Motto).*

70

**Prayer to Jesus the Listener**

Jesus the Listener, I come to You because I need You to look upon me and love me. You know me better than anyone. You know my joys and my sorrows, my struggles and my suffering. May your merciful glance inspire me with perseverance in accepting everything for love of You. I shall not depart from your presence without saying with the Psalmist: "I love the Lord because he has heard my voice in supplication, because he has inclined his ear to me the day I called" (Psalm 116:1-2). I ask this through the infinite merits of your Passion and Death. Amen.

*The Authors*

> *"The message of the cross is complete absurdity to those who are headed for ruin, but to us who are experiencing salvation it is the power of God" (1 Corinthians 1:18).*